Christmas in Germany

by Kristin Thoennes

Consultants:
Instructors of the Language Services Department
Germanic-American Institute

Bridgestone Books

an imprint of Capstone Press
Mankato, Minnesota

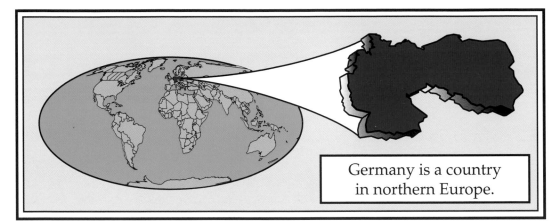

Germany is a country
in northern Europe.

Bridgestone Books are published by Capstone Press
151 Good Counsel Drive, P.O. Box 669, Mankato, Minnesota 56002
http://www.capstone-press.com
Copyright © 1999 Capstone Press. All rights reserved.

Library of Congress Cataloging-in-Publication Data
Thoennes, Kristin.
    Christmas in Germany/by Kristin Thoennes.
    p. cm.—(Christmas around the world)
    Includes bibliographical references and index.
    Summary: An overview of the symbols, celebrations, decorations, food, and songs that are part of
Christmas in Germany.
    ISBN 0-7368-0089-1
    1. Christmas—Germany—Juvenile literature. 2. Germany—Social life and customs—Juvenile
literature. [1. Christmas—Germany. 2. Germany—Social life and customs. 3. Holidays.] I. Title. II. Series.
GT4987.49.T56 1999
394.2663'0943—dc21

        98-16202
        CIP
        AC

Editorial Credits
Michelle L. Norstad, editor; James Franklin, cover designer and illustrator; Sheri Gosewisch, photo researcher
Photo credits
Gerhard Gscheidle, 4, 12
Keystone, 10, 16, 18
Photo Researchers/David Kraus, cover; Josef Ege, 20
Trip Photo Library/F. Lulinksi, 8, 14
Unicorn Stock Photos/D & I MacDonald, 6

2 3 4 5 6 04 03 02 01 00

Table of Contents

Christmas in Germany

Many people around the world celebrate Christmas. Celebrate means to do something enjoyable on a special occasion. People in different countries celebrate Christmas in different ways.

Germany is a country in northern Europe. People from Germany are Germans. They speak the German language. Their Christmas greeting is Fröhliche Weihnachten (FROH-lik-uh VEYE-nahkt-en). It means Merry Christmas.

Germans celebrate Christmas Day on December 25. But Germans begin celebrating the Christmas season four weeks before Christmas Day. The Christmas season in Germany ends on January 6. Germans call this day Epiphany or Three King's Day.

The weather in Germany at Christmas time is cold. The temperatures are near freezing on some days. Snow covers much of the country.

Germans begin celebrating the Christmas season four weeks before Christmas Day.

The First Christmas

Many people who celebrate Christmas are Christians. A Christian is a person who follows the teachings of Jesus Christ. Christians celebrate Jesus' birthday on Christmas Day.

Christians tell the story of the day Jesus was born. Mary was Jesus' mother. Joseph was her husband. Mary and Joseph traveled to the town of Bethlehem. They could not find a room at any of the inns. An inn is like a hotel. Mary and Joseph had to stay in a building for animals called a stable. Jesus was born in the stable.

Jesus' first bed was a manger. A manger is a food box for animals. Mary and Joseph put straw in the manger. The straw kept Jesus warm.

Three kings saw a bright star the night Jesus was born. The kings followed the star to the stable. They brought gifts for Jesus.

Jesus was born in a stable.

Christmas Trees

Christmas trees are symbols of Christmas in Germany. A symbol is an object that reminds people of something important. The German word for Christmas tree is Tannenbaum (TAH-nuhn-bawm). Germans were the first people to use Christmas trees.

Many stories tell about how evergreen trees became Christmas trees. Most evergreen trees are pine trees. One story says Germans believed both evergreen trees and lights kept away bad spirits. During the 12 days of Christmas, Germans put candles on the evergreens to keep away bad spirits.

Another story tells about a German minister named Martin Luther. A minister is a person who leads a church. Martin walked in a forest one starry Christmas Eve. He thought the evergreens and stars were beautiful. Martin cut down an evergreen tree and put candles on it. Martin thought the candlelight looked like stars.

Christmas trees are symbols of Christmas in Germany.

Decorations

Germans put many types of decorations on Christmas trees. They use thin pieces of shiny metal or paper called tinsel. They put candles, stars, or angels on Christmas trees. Germans also may use baked decorations called Lebkuchen (LAYB-kook-en).

Many Germans hang strings of lights outside. They hang lights on lampposts, houses, and store fronts.

Germans decorate with Advent wreaths. An Advent wreath is a circle of greenery with four candles. People light one candle the first week. They light two candles the second week and three the third week. People light all four candles the fourth week.

The Advent calendar is another popular German decoration. An Advent calendar has doors on it. Each door covers one day from December 1 to Christmas Day. Children open one door each day. Pictures, treats, or small gifts may lie behind the doors.

Germans decorate with Advent wreaths.

Christmas Celebrations

Many Germans celebrate Christmas at Christmas markets. People hear songs and music at these markets. Germans can watch puppet shows and plays. Shoppers can buy food, toys, and Christmas decorations.

Germans celebrate many holidays during the Christmas season. They celebrate Saint Nicholas Day on December 6. Saint Nicholas is the saint for children.

The Christmas tree is an important part of German celebrations. Parents spend Christmas Eve decorating the tree. Children wait in another room until they hear a bell. Then parents bring their children into the room. The children see their presents under the decorated tree.

Germans also celebrate the Second Day of Christmas. This holiday is on December 26. Many Germans spend this day with family and friends.

Germans celebrate New Year's Day on January 1. People welcome the new year with parties, fireworks, and music.

Many Germans celebrate Christmas at Christmas markets.

Saint Nicholas

Many German children believe in Saint Nicholas. Saint Nicholas wears a red robe and a pointed hat. He also has a white beard and carries a cane. Children leave their shoes out for Saint Nicholas on December 5. The next day, they find their shoes filled with toys and treats.

Some children also believe in the Weihnachtsmann (VEYE-nakts-mahn). Weihnachtsmann means Christmas man. He looks like Saint Nicholas. The Weihnachtsmann brings gifts on Christmas Eve.

Some children write letters to the Cristkind (KRISS-kind). The Cristkind is the baby Jesus. Children may write letters to ask for gifts. Some children put the letters on a windowsill. Sometimes children make their letters sparkle. They put glue on the letters. Then they sprinkle sugar on the glue.

The Weihnachtsmann brings gifts on Christmas Eve.

Christmas Presents

Germans give presents at Christmas time. Presents remind Germans of the three kings' gifts. The three kings brought presents to Jesus when he was born.

Family members give each other presents on Christmas Eve. Some families read about Jesus' birth before opening presents. Families do this to remember Jesus on his birthday.

Germans spend Christmas Day and December 26 with friends and family. Children receive presents from aunts, uncles, and grandparents. They also may receive presents from friends.

German children receive many kinds of presents. They may receive dolls, trains, or jewelry such as rings and necklaces. They also may receive clothes, books, or games.

German children receive many kinds of presents.

Holiday Foods

Families in Germany eat many different foods during the Christmas season. Some families eat roast goose or roast pork. Others may eat turkey or duck. Carp is another popular Christmas food. Carp is fish.

A popular treat in Germany is Lebkuchen. Lebkuchen is gingerbread. Some people use Lebkuchen as decorations. They make Lebkuchen cookies shaped like stars or bells. They hang the Lebkuchen cookies on Christmas trees.

Gingerbread houses are popular in Germany. Germans make them with Lebkuchen. They decorate the gingerbread houses with frosting and candy.

Another popular treat is marzipan (MAIR-zi-pan). Marzipan is a candy made of roasted almonds and sugar. Many Germans enjoy the taste of marzipan.

Gingerbread houses are very popular in Germany.

Christmas Songs

Germans wrote many Christmas songs. Several are popular all over the world. One song is "Oh Christmas Tree." Another song is "Silent Night, Holy Night." "Hark! The Herald Angels Sing" is also a Christmas song from Germany.

Christmas caroling is popular in Germany. Years ago, poor Germans caroled from house to house. They sang outside each house. People sometimes gave the singers small gifts. Many Germans still enjoy Christmas caroling today.

Many German town bands play songs during the Christmas season. The bands play music in town squares. They also play songs in churches.

Many Germans go to church services on Christmas Eve. They sing songs together at church services. They also listen to music.

Many Germans go to church services on Christmas Eve.

Read More

Christmas in Today's Germany. Christmas around the World from World Book. Chicago: World Book, 1993.

Lankford, Mary. *Christmas around the World.* New York: Morrow Junior Books, 1995.

Naythons, Matthew. *Christmas around the World.* San Francisco: Collins Publishers, 1996.

Useful Addresses and Internet Sites

The German Embassy
4645 Reservoir Road
Washington, DC 20007

Germanic-American Institute
301 Summit Avenue
St. Paul, MN 55102

Christmas in Germany
http://www.germanembassyottawa.org/Christmas/index.html
Christmas in Germany
http://www.germany-info.org/gnew/christmas/christmas.htm
Santa's Favorites: Around the World
http://www.santas.net/germanchristmas.htm

Index